New Series!
Discover America

Reading Level: Grade 5
Interest Level: Grades 4-7

The United States of America is made up of many states an
America series uses exciting images and informative text to
history, landscape, and identity of each U.S. state, territory, a

Publisher: Weigl Publishers • Discount: 30% off list
Binding: Reinforced Library • Size: 7½ x 10 • Pages: 48
Features: Full-Color Photographs, Maps, Charts, Timelines, Glossary, Index

___	**WEK197 Discover America (52 vols.)**	**1,091.48**
___	WE8150 Alabama: The Heart of Dixie/Parker, 17	20.99
___	WE8181 Alaska: The Last Frontier/Strudwick, 17	20.99
___	WE8211 Arizona: The Grand Canyon State/Craats, 17	20.99
___	WE8242 Arkansas: The Natural State/Pezzi, 17	20.99
___	WE8273 California: The Golden State/Parker, 17	20.99
___	WE8303 Colorado: The Centennial State/McLuskey, 17	20.99
___	WE8334 Connecticut: The Constitution State/Webster, 17	20.99
___	WE8365 Delaware: The First State/Winans, 17	20.99
___	WE8396 District of Columbia: The Nation's Capital/Thomas, 17	20.99
___	WE8426 Florida: The Sunshine State/Sullivan, 17	20.99
___	WE8457 Georgia: The Peach State/Nault, 17	20.99
___	WE8488 Hawai'i: The Aloha State/Foran, 17	20.99
___	WE8518 Idaho: The Gem State/Foran, 17	20.99
___	WE8549 Illinois: The Prairie State/Craats, 17	20.99
___	WE8570 Indiana: The Hoosier State/Craats, 17	20.99
___	WE8600 Iowa: The Hawkeye State/Winans, 17	20.99
___	WE8631 Kansas: The Sunflower State/Nault, 17	20.99
___	WE8662 Kentucky: The Bluegrass State/Evdokimoff, 17	20.99
___	WE8693 Louisiana: The Pelican State/Johnstone, 17	20.99
___	WE8723 Maine: The Pine Tree State/Foran, 17	20.99
___	WE8754 Maryland: The Old Line State/Craats, 17	20.99
___	WE8785 Massachusetts: The Bay State/Pezzi, 17	20.99
___	WE8815 Michigan: The Wolverine State/Craats, 17	20.99
___	WE8846 Minnesota: The North Star State/Purslow, 17	20.99
___	WE8877 Mississippi: The Magnolia State/Foran, 17	20.99
___	WE8907 Missouri: The Show Me State/Evdokimoff, 17	20.99
___	WE8938 Montana: The Treasure State/McLuskey, 17	20.99
___	WE8969 Nebraska: The Cornhusker State/Foran, 17	20.99
___	WE8990 Nevada: The Silver State/McLuskey, 17	20.99
___	WE9027 New Hampshire: The Granite State/Craats, 17	20.99
___	WE9058 New Jersey: The Garden State/Nault, 17	20.99
___	WE9089 New Mexico: The Land of Enchantment/Craats, 17	20.99
___	WE9119 New York: The Empire State/Lawton, 17	20.99
___	WE9140 North Carolina: The Tar Heel State/Foran, 17	20.99
___	WE9171 North Dakota: The Peace Garden State/Watson, 17	20.99
___	WE9201 Ohio: The Buckeye State/Lawton, 17	20.99
___	WE9232 Oklahoma: The Sooner State/Strudwick, 17	20.99
___	WE9263 Oregon: The Beaver State/Winans, 17	20.99
___	WE9294 Pennsylvania: The Keystone State/Evdokimoff, 17	20.99
___	WE9324 Puerto Rico: Isle of Enchantment/Goldsworthy, 17	20.99
___	WE9355 Rhode Island: The Ocean State/Winans, 17	20.99
___	WE9386 South Carolina: The Palmetto State/Parker, 17	20.99
___	WE9416 South Dakota: The Mount Rushmore State/Strudwick, 17	20.99
___	WE9447 Tennessee: The Volunteer State/Semchuk, 17	20.99
___	WE9478 Texas: The Lone Star State/Parker, 17	20.99
___	WE9508 Utah: The Beehive State/Parker, 17	20.99
___	WE9539 Vermont: The Green Mountain State/Foran, 17	20.99
___	WE9560 Virginia: The Old Dominion/Parker, 17	20.99
___	WE9591 Washington: The Evergreen State/Strudwick, 17	20.99
___	WE9621 West Virginia: The Mountain State/Lawton, 17	20.99
___	WE9652 Wisconsin: The Badger State/Parker, 17	20.99
___	WE9683 Wyoming: The Equality State/Parker, 17	20.99

DISCOVER AMERICA

VIRGINIA

Janice Parker

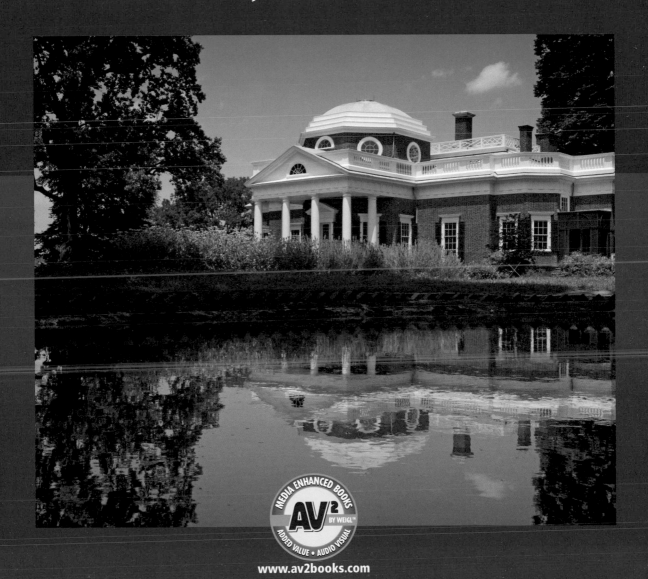

AV² provides enriched content that supplements and complements this book. Weigl's AV² books strive to create inspired learning and engage young minds in a total learning experience.

Your AV² Media Enhanced books come alive with...

Audio
Listen to sections of the book read aloud.

Key Words
Study vocabulary, and complete a matching word activity.

Video
Watch informative video clips.

Quizzes
Test your knowledge.

Embedded Weblinks
Gain additional information for research.

Slide Show
View images and captions, and prepare a presentation.

Try This!
Complete activities and hands-on experiments.

... and much, much more!

Go to **www.av2books.com**, and enter this book's unique code.

BOOK CODE

S 2 3 3 8 7 8

AV² by Weigl brings you media enhanced books that support active learning.

Published by AV² by Weigl
350 5th Avenue, 59th Floor
New York, NY 10118
Website: www.av2books.com

Library of Congress Cataloging-in-Publication Data
Names: Parker, Janice, author.
Title: Virginia : the Old Dominion / Janice Parker.
Description: AV2 by Weigl : New York, NY, 2016. | Series: Discover America | Includes index.
Identifiers: LCCN 2015048046 (print) | LCCN 2015049104 (ebook) | ISBN 9781489649560 (hard cover : alk. paper) | ISBN 9781489649577 (soft cover : alk. paper) | ISBN 9781489649584 (Multi-User eBook)
Subjects: LCSH: Virginia--Juvenile literature.
Classification: LCC F226.3 .P374 2016 (print) | LCC F226.3 (ebook) | DDC 975.5--dc23
LC record available at http://lccn.loc.gov/2015048046

Printed in the United States of America, in Brainerd, Minnesota
1 2 3 4 5 6 7 8 9 20 19 18 17 16

052016
270516

Project Coordinator Heather Kissock
Art Director Terry Paulhus

Photo Credits
Every reasonable effort has been made to trace ownership and to obtain permission to reprint copyright material. The publisher would be pleased to have any errors or omissions brought to their attention so that they may be corrected in subsequent printings. The publisher acknowledges Getty

VIRGINIA

Contents

STATE TREE
Flowering Dogwood

STATE BIRD
Cardinal

STATE FLOWER
Dogwood

STATE FLAG
Virginia

STATE INSECT
Tiger Swallowtail Butterfly

STATE SEAL
Virginia

Nicknames
The Old Dominion

Motto
Sic Semper Tyrannis
(Thus Ever to Tyrants)

Song
no official state song

Population
(2010 Census) 8,001,024
Ranked 12th state

Entered the Union
June 25, 1788, as the 10th state

Discover Virginia

Virginia is located on the eastern coast of the United States. It is bordered by Maryland and Washington, D.C. to the northeast. Chesapeake Bay and the Atlantic Ocean are to the east. North Carolina and Tennessee are to the south. Kentucky is to the west, and West Virginia to the northwest.

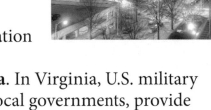

Virginia's economy is closely tied to that of the nation as a whole. A large and fast-growing part of the state's population lives in northeastern Virginia, in the Washington, D.C., **metropolitan area**. In Virginia, U.S. military bases, along with federal, state, and local governments, provide jobs for nearly one-fifth of the state's non-farm labor force.

For visitors, there are a variety of theme parks and animal parks in the state. Busch Gardens, in Williamsburg, and Fort Chiswell Animal Park, in Max Meadows, are just two of these attractions in Virginia. In McGaheysville, the Massanutten indoor and outdoor water park boasts eight indoor water slides and an 80,000-square-foot outdoor water park area.

Virginia also features a variety of national parks, monuments, and historic sites. The Blue Ridge Mountains span both Virginia and North Carolina. Assateague Island is an ever-changing island off Virginia's coast that features salt marshes, coastal bays, and sandy beaches. Civil War battlegrounds Fredericksburg and Spotsylvania have been preserved as national parks.

The Land

The Appalachian Mountains, thought to be among the oldest mountains in North America, dominate much of western Virginia.

Thomas Jefferson founded the **University of Virginia** in **1819.**

The **House of Burgesses**, a branch of Virginia's early government, was the **first elected legislative body** in North America.

Beginnings

Although Virginia is nicknamed the Old Dominion, it is often referred to as the "Birthplace of Presidents." Four of the first five U.S. presidents came from Virginia. George Washington, Thomas Jefferson, James Madison, and James Monroe all held the nation's highest office between 1789 and 1825.

Virginia played a crucial role in the American Revolutionary War. Thomas Jefferson was responsible for writing the Declaration of Independence in 1776. Five years later, the decisive battle of the American Revolutionary War was fought on Virginia soil, at Yorktown. U.S. and French troops, led by General George Washington, surrounded the British during the siege of Yorktown. The British surrendered after 20 days. On June 25, 1788, Virginia became the tenth state to **ratify** the U.S. Constitution and join the Union.

Virginia **seceded** from the Union in April 1861. Richmond served as the capital of the Confederacy from June 1861 to April 1865, and much of the Civil War was fought on Virginia soil. Residents of Virginia's western counties had differing views from residents in the rest of the state. They had not wanted to leave the Union and voted to form a new state. One-third of Virginia became West Virginia in June 1863. The Confederate army, led by Virginian Robert E. Lee, surrendered to Union troops at Appomattox Court House, Virginia, on April 9, 1865. Virginia was readmitted to the Union in January 1870.

After four long years of bloody war, Confederate General Robert E. Lee surrendered to Union commander Ulysses S. Grant at Appomattox Court House. His surrender effectively ended the Civil War.

Where is VIRGINIA?

Roughly triangular in shape, Virginia has a total area of 42,775 square miles. Land makes up about 93 percent of the total, and water accounts for the remaining 7 percent. Coastal waters make up more than half of the state's water area. Virginia's coast is highly irregular. Including offshore islands, bays, and tidal areas of rivers and creeks, the state's shoreline measures 3,315 miles.

WEST VIRGINIA

United States Map

Virginia

Alaska   Hawai'i

MAP LEGEND

- ▨ Virginia
- ☆ Capital City
- ▲ Hampton Roads
- ■ Chincoteague Island
- ▮ Great Dismal Swamp
- ▢ Bordering States
- ▢ Water

NORTH

① Richmond

Located on the James River, Richmond has been the capital of Virginia since 1780. It also served as the capital of the Confederacy during the Civil War. Today, Richmond has more than 204,000 residents and is Virginia's fifth-largest city. Visitors can experience the Edgar Allen Poe Museum.

② Hampton Roads

Hampton Roads is both a bay and a city. Since colonial times, the city has been built around the military. Today, it is home to the oldest navy shipyard in the country. Guests to the area can visit the Hampton Roads Naval Museum. It highlights 234 years of U.S. naval history.

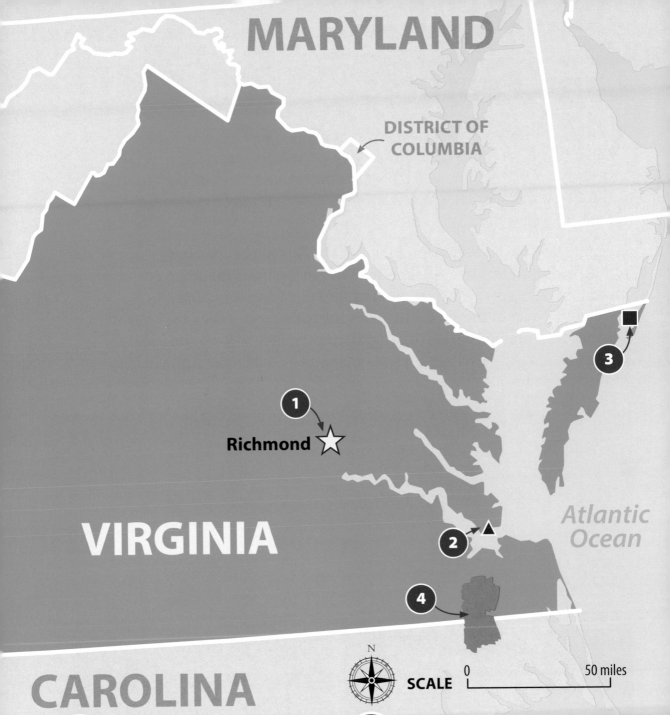

MARYLAND

DISTRICT OF
COLUMBIA

1 Richmond

VIRGINIA

2

3

4

Atlantic
Ocean

CAROLINA

N

SCALE

0   50 miles

3 Chincoteague Island

Perhaps best known through Marguerite Henry's book *Misty of Chincoteague*, Chincoteague is a relaxing tourist destination. It is the site of the annual pony penning, when wild horses on nearby Assateague Island are guided across the channel.

4 Great Dismal Swamp

Although it once covered about 2,000 square miles, the Great Dismal Swamp now covers 750 square miles. It contains Lake Drummond, the largest natural lake in Virginia, and is only 6 feet deep. The Great Dismal Swamp is home to rare birds and many venomous snakes.

Land Features

Virginia consists of several distinct regions. The Eastern Shore, at the southern tip of the Delmarva Peninsula, is separated from the rest of Virginia by Chesapeake Bay. Extending inland from the coast is the Coastal Plain, a flat and swampy region. This area is sometimes called the Tidewater.

West of the Coastal Plain is the Piedmont. This region has low, rolling hills and fertile soils. The Blue Ridge region is made up of mountains that form a ridge crossing the state from northeast to southwest. West of the Blue Ridge lies the Ridge and Valley region and another mountainous area, the Appalachian Plateau. Both the Blue Ridge and the Appalachian Plateau are parts of the larger Appalachian Mountain chain.

Potomac River

The Potomac River separates Arlington, Virginia, from Washington, D.C.

Shenandoah National Park

Located in northern Virginia, Shenandoah National Park includes the 4,050-foot-high summit of Hawksbill Mountain.

Chesapeake Bay

Chesapeake Bay extends about 200 miles from Havre de Grace, Maryland, to Virginia Beach. The bay has a surface area of nearly 4,500 square miles.

Smith Mountain Lake

Smith Mountain Lake was developed by a power company to provide electricity, drinking water, and recreational opportunities for surrounding areas of southwestern Virginia.

Climate

While Virginia generally has hot, humid summers and mild, wet winters, the climate varies across the state. Southeastern Virginia, near the coast, has a mild climate with very little snowfall. The northwestern part of the state has colder winters, with greater snowfall in elevated areas.

Average temperatures in Richmond range from 36° Fahrenheit in January to 78°F in July. Averages in the Piedmont region are usually more extreme in each season. Record temperatures in the state include a high of 110°F in 1954 and a low of –30°F in 1985.

Average Annual Precipitation Across Virginia

The average annual precipitation varies for different areas across Virginia. How does location affect the amount of precipitation an area receives?

LEGEND

Average Annual Precipitation (in inches) 1961–1990

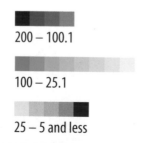

200 – 100.1

100 – 25.1

25 – 5 and less

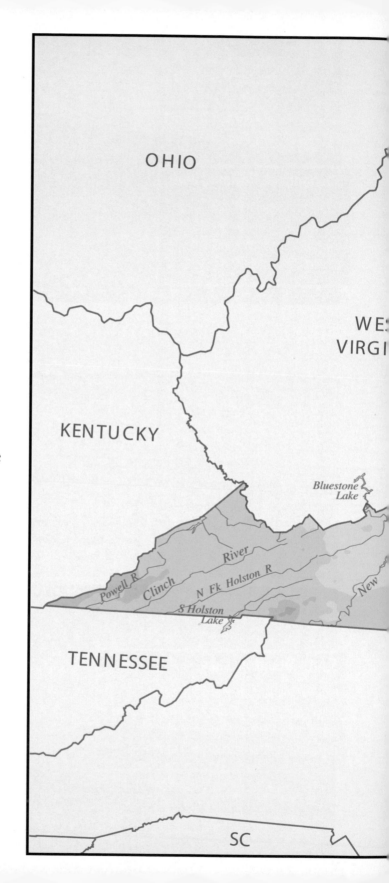

OHIO

WEST VIRGINIA

KENTUCKY

Bluestone Lake

River

Powell R.   Clinch   N Fk Holston R   New

S Holston Lake

TENNESSEE

SC

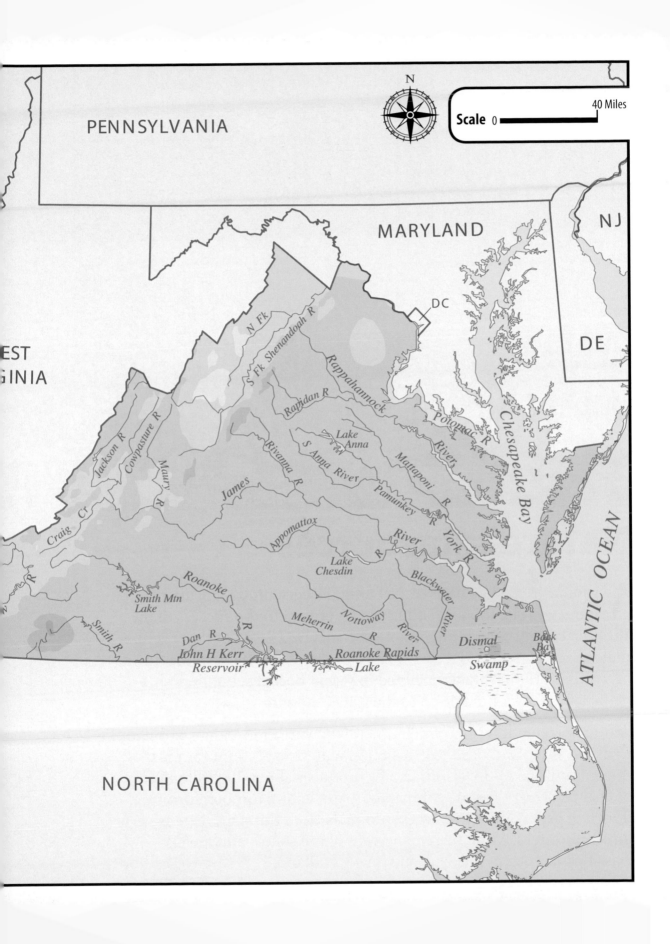

PENNSYLVANIA

N

Scale 0 ━━━ 40 Miles

MARYLAND

NJ

DC

DE

WEST
VIRGINIA

N Fk

S Fk Shenandoah R

Rappahannock

Rapidan R

Potomac R

Lake
Anna

Chesapeake Bay

Cowpasture R

Jackson R

Maury R

Rivanna R

S Anna River

Mattaponi R

Pamunkey

River

York R

James

Craig Cr

R

Appomattox

Lake
Chesdin

River

R

Blackwater River

ATLANTIC OCEAN

Roanoke

Smith Mtn
Lake

Meherrin

Nottoway River

R

R

Dismal

Back
Bay

Smith R

Dan R

R

John H Kerr
Reservoir

Roanoke Rapids
Lake

Swamp

NORTH CAROLINA

Although not as important to Virginia as other Southern states, cotton is still a lucrative crop for the state.

Nature's Resources

Virginia's rich soils have helped to make agriculture a primary industry. The tobacco industry was crucial to the success of the Virginia colony, which might not have survived without the revenue that tobacco sales produced. Tobacco growing and the manufacturing of tobacco products have declined in recent decades, but they still make a notable contribution to the state economy.

Annual production of nonfuel minerals is worth more than $1 billion. Crushed stone and other construction materials account for most of the output. The Old Dominion also produces about 30 million tons of coal per year. Virginia companies manufacture lumber, furniture, flooring, paper, and other wood products from the state's extensive forest resources. More than 60 percent of the state's land area is classified as commercially productive woodland.

Vineyards have been present in Virginia since the seventeenth century.

Early European settlers learned tobacco farming from local Native American groups. Tobacco quickly became the cornerstone of Virginia's economy.

Vegetation

Hardwood trees such as hickories, maples, white oaks, and red oaks are abundant in Virginia's forests. Other trees commonly found in the Old Dominion include white pines, sycamores, and willows. In the wetlands, tupelos, bald cypresses, and swamp oaks grow. Dogwood can be found throughout most of the state, while azaleas, mountain laurels, and rhododendrons are common in the mountain regions.

The Virginia Native Plant Society was founded in 1982 to help conserve plants that are native to the state. The society also chooses a wildflower of the year. One popular wildflower is the trailing arbutus, commonly known as the mayflower.

Blanketflower

This native flower is both heat and drought tolerant. It is popular in home gardens throughout Virginia.

Tupelo

Prized for its fiery red color in autumn, the tupelo tree is also valuable as a source of pulp for paper and wood for carvers.

Hickory

The hard, strong wood of the hickory tree is used for baseball bats, skis, and tool handles, among other products.

Mayflower

The mayflower, or trailing arbutus, is a small evergreen shrub that grows in forested areas.

Wildlife

Although many large mammals once lived in Virginia, only the black bear and the white-tailed deer still roam the state. Smaller mammals such as beavers, muskrats, skunks, otters, foxes, and raccoons are more plentiful. Common reptiles and **amphibians** include the box turtle and the bullfrog, and more than 30 species of snake live in Virginia. Nuthatches and woodpeckers live in the state's forests. Gulls, herons, and bitterns reside around lakes and ponds. Birds of prey that live in the state include the bald eagle, the peregrine falcon, and the osprey.

Beaver

Found throughout Virginia, especially where aspen trees are plentiful, beavers prefer smooth-bottomed streams to ones that are steep and rocky.

Northern Copperhead

The poisonous northern copperhead is found throughout the state at elevations below 3,000 feet.

White-tailed Deer

Wildlife management efforts have succeeded in boosting Virginia's deer population from an estimated 150,000 in 1950 to nearly 1 million in recent years.

Cardinal

Found throughout the state, the cardinal has also been called the "Virginia red bird" and the "Virginia nightingale."

Economy

Virginia Beach

More than 2.7 million people visit Virginia Beach per year.

Tourism

The beauty of Virginia Beach once prompted an early explorer to exclaim, "Heaven and Earth never agreed better to frame a place for man's **habitations** than Virginia." Today, Virginia Beach is the largest city in the state. It is also one of the most popular vacation destinations on the east coast.

Tourists are also drawn to Virginia's many historic attractions. Battlefields from the American Revolutionary War and the Civil War are scattered across the state. One of Virginia's most treasured sites is Monticello, the home of Thomas Jefferson. For more than 40 years, Jefferson built and rebuilt the house into one of the most impressive homes in the world.

Mabry Mill

Located along the Blue Ridge Parkway, Mabry Mill features a working, water-powered grist mill and demonstrations of old-time Appalachian crafts.

Colonial Williamsburg

Dedicated in 1934, the restored House of Burgesses is the centerpiece of Colonial Williamsburg. Virginia's legislature continues to meet here instead of Richmond on special ceremonial occasions.

Arlington National Cemetery

Each year, about 6,900 military veterans and others are honored with burial at Arlington National Cemetery.

Virginian fishermen sail the Chesapeake Bay and Atlantic Ocean looking for flounder, bass, oysters, soft clams, and crab.

Primary Industries

Agriculture was once the dominant industry in Virginia. Today, it contributes less than 1 percent to the state economy. Principal agricultural products include **broiler chickens**, eggs, cattle, greenhouse or nursery goods, milk, fodder crops, tobacco, turkeys, and peanuts.

Chesapeake Bay provides Virginia with many different types of fish. More than 200 million clams and nearly 5 million oysters are harvested annually. Crabs, sea scallops, flounder, and striped bass are also important to commercial fishing in the state.

Traditionally, tobacco products were among Virginia's most valuable manufactured goods. Today, the state also makes electronic components, chemical products, processed foods, clothing, transportation equipment, and furniture, as well as other wood products. Virginia's top exports include machinery, coal, transportation equipment, plastics, paper, optical and medical instruments, and chemicals.

Northrop Grumman Shipbuilding, in Newport News, is one of the **largest shipbuilders** in the world and builds nuclear-powered aircraft carriers and submarines.

The first **peanuts** grown in the United States were cultivated in Virginia.

Value of Goods and Services (in Millions of Dollars)

In 1800, the federal and state governments were very small, and agriculture was Virginia's main economic activity. How has the state economy changed since that time?

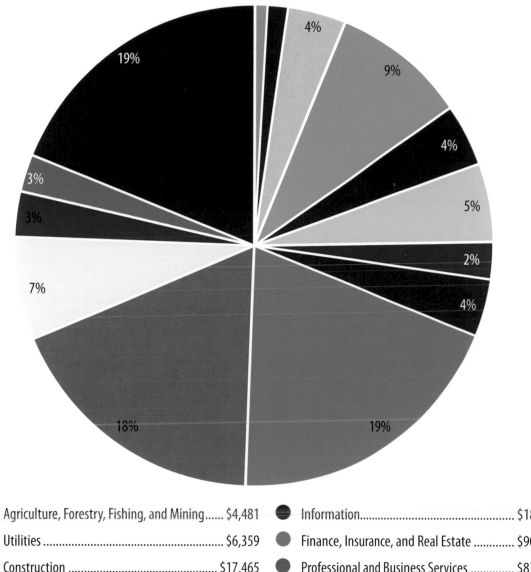

● Agriculture, Forestry, Fishing, and Mining	$4,481	● Information	$18,393
● Utilities	$6,359	● Finance, Insurance, and Real Estate	$90,025
● Construction	$17,465	● Professional and Business Services	$83,446
● Manufacturing	$43,101	● Educational, Health and Social Services	$31,822
● Wholesale Trade	$19,028	● Recreation and Accommodation	$14,087
● Retail Trade	$24,379	● Other Services	$11,875
● Transportation and Warehousing	$11,397	● Government	$87,001

Goods and Services

The federal government employs many Virginians and is essential to the state's economy. The Pentagon, in Arlington, is the headquarters of the U.S. Department of Defense. The department employs about 23,000 military and **civilian** workers. They receive support from another 3,000 people who work at the site in non-defense jobs.

Many important military bases are located in Virginia, including the world's largest naval station, at Norfolk. The U.S. Marine Corps Base in Quantico is where all U.S. Marines receive their basic training. The Quantico facility also hosts the training academy of the Federal Bureau of Investigation, or FBI.

Norfolk has been an important port in Virginia since the 1600s. Today, commercial ships and U.S. naval vessels, including aircraft carriers and destroyers, sail into harbor.

The Library of Virginia, in Richmond, contains the **archives** of the Commonwealth of Virginia. Leading public colleges and universities in the state include the University of Virginia in Charlottesville, Virginia Tech in Blacksburg, and the College of William and Mary in Williamsburg. Founded in 1839, the state-supported Virginia Military Institute is located in Lexington.

Founded in 1693, the College of William & Mary is the second-oldest institution of higher education in the United States, after Harvard.

Trainees spend 10 weeks at the FBI Academy in Quantico before being admitted into the Bureau.

Pocahontas's name has become synonymous with early U.S. history and the struggle between European colonists and Native Americans.

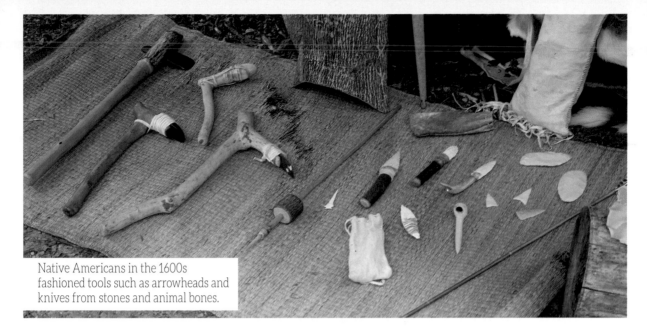

Native Americans in the 1600s fashioned tools such as arrowheads and knives from stones and animal bones.

Native Americans

Prehistoric Native Americans lived in the Virginia region at least 16,000 years ago. These early peoples used tools made of stone and relied mainly on hunting for their food. About 3,000 years ago, some groups began to settle in villages. They hunted, fished, and grew food crops such as corn and squash, as well as tobacco. They made ceramic bowls and other pottery, and traded with nearby groups. These Native Americans mostly spoke languages belonging to the Algonquian, Iroquoian, and Siouan language groups.

Probably about 50,000 Native Americans were living in the region by the 1600s, when the first European settlers arrived. Early European settlers came in contact with Native Americans of the Powhatan Confederacy, which included at least 30 Algonquian-speaking groups that lived near the coast. The confederacy had been founded by and named for a powerful chief, Powhatan.

Violence erupted between settlers and Native Americans, and in 1613 the British colonists captured Powhatan's daughter, Pocahontas. She married a British settler, John Rolfe, in 1614. The marriage brought peace to the area for several years. Fighting resumed between the Powhatan Confederacy and the British a few years after her death in 1617.

Exploring the Land

In 1494, the King of Great Britain commissioned Italian explorer Giovanni Caboto, known to history as John Cabot, to search for new land in the west. Cabot may have been the first European to see Virginia when he reached the shore in 1497, but he died on his second journey to the New World in 1498. In 1524, the Italian explorer Giovanni da Verrazzano explored Virginia's coast for France.

In 1606, three ships carrying 104 passengers from the Virginia Company of London traveled from Great Britain to North America. The Virginia Company had been created to settle Virginia. After arriving in May 1607, the voyagers on the *Susan Constant*, *Godspeed*, and *Discovery* founded a settlement called Jamestown.

Timeline of Settlement

Further Colonization

1676 Colonial authorities put down Bacon's Rebellion, a settler uprising.

1619 An elected legislature, the House of Burgesses, begins meeting. The first shipload of Africans arrives.

1693 Virginia's first college, the College of William and Mary, is founded in Williamsburg.

1607 British settlers found a colony at Jamestown.

1524 Sailing for France, Italian navigator Giovanni da Verrazzano explores the Virginia coastline.

1699 Williamsburg becomes Virginia's colonial capital.

Early Exploration and Settlement

When Sir Thomas Gates arrived in Jamestown in 1610 to become governor of the colony, he found only 60 surviving settlers. Conflict with the Powhata Native Americans, along with a drought, made life difficult for the colonists, and many starved to death. Just as the settlers were about to abandon the colony, Sir Thomas West, baron de la Warr, arrived and took control of the Jamestown settlement. Gradually, life in Jamestown began to improve.

1783 The defeat of the British at Yorktown secures a U.S. victory in the American Revolutionary War.

Statehood and Civil War

1776 Another Virginian, Thomas Jefferson, drafts the Declaration of Independence.

1788 Virginia is the 10th state to ratify the Constitution and join the Union.

1775 Early in the American Revolutionary War, George Washington, a Virginian, becomes commander-in-chief of the Continental Army.

1789–1825 Four of the nation's first five presidents, including Washington and Jefferson, are Virginians.

Independence and American Revolutionary War

1861–1865 Virginia secedes from the Union, and Richmond becomes the capital of the Confederacy. The Civil War ends with Confederate General Robert E. Lee's surrender at Appomattox Court House.

At first, the settlers at Jamestown struggled to survive. Many were nobles, merchants, or soldiers, and did not know how to farm.

The First Settlers

Colonial Virginia was built on tobacco. Native American groups had been using tobacco as a medicine and in ceremonies for at least 2,000 years. John Rolfe, a colonist who came to Virginia in 1610, began to grow a type of tobacco from the West Indies that had a mild taste. Growers in Virginia exported it to Great Britain and the rest of Europe, where it became very popular.

The settlement soon began to thrive. By 1619, it had its own government, with a two-chamber legislature. In 1624, Virginia became a royal colony.

Africans were first brought to Jamestown in 1619 as **indentured servants**. Legalized slavery was not introduced for several decades. Black slaves were the foundation of the **plantation** agriculture that began in the Tidewater region and spread into the Piedmont.

In 1676, a group of settlers led by the British aristocrat and colonist Nathaniel Bacon rose up against Virginia's colonial government in what is known as Bacon's Rebellion. The group opposed many of Governor William Berkeley's policies. They disliked the governor's refusal to call elections, his lack of a plan to combat Native American attacks, and his favoritism toward new, wealthy colonists. The rebels attacked and burned Jamestown, forcing Berkeley to flee. When Bacon died unexpectedly, Berkeley returned, reclaimed power, and hanged many of the rebels without trials.

Nathaniel Bacon's 1677 rebellion against Governor Berkeley was an important early stepping stone towards democracy in the United States.

By the end of the 1600s, Dutch and British slave ships were bringing slaves from West Africa. They were used primarily on tobacco plantations to replace indentured servants.

History Makers

More than any other state, Virginia provided the talented and courageous leaders who transformed the original 13 colonies into a free and independent nation. More recently, inspirational educators, creative musical artists, and pioneering athletes have called Virginia their home. It has also been home to many civil rights activists, and influential politicians continue to spring from Virginia.

George Washington (1732–1799)

Born in Westmoreland County, George Washington is celebrated as the "Father of His Country." He served with the British Army in the 1750s, but later became a strong supporter of U.S. independence, commanding the Continental Army during the American Revolutionary War. The country's first president, he served two terms, from 1789 to 1797, before retiring to his home in Mount Vernon.

Ella Baker (1903–1986)

A civil and human rights activist, Ella Baker worked tirelessly to advocate for equality. She spent her life inspiring many African Americans to get involved, and helped to build many of the major organizations of the time. Today, the Ella Baker Center for Human Rights continues her fight.

James Madison (1751–1836)

The son of a Virginia tobacco planter, James Madison grew up to become one of the 18th century's greatest political thinkers. Known as the "Father of the Constitution," he had a major role in writing and explaining the nation's founding document. He served from 1809 to 1817 as the fourth U.S. president, leading the country through the War of 1812.

James Monroe (1758–1831)

A lawyer, legislator, and follower of Thomas Jefferson, James Monroe served as the nation's fifth president, from 1817 to 1825. Monroe famously declared that the United States would resist any future efforts by Europe to colonize or interfere with states in the Americas.

Booker T. Washington (1856–1915)

Born a slave in southwestern Virginia, Booker T. Washington became an influential educator and African American leader. He believed education for freed slaves should emphasize the practical skills they needed to advance economically. His book *Up from Slavery* was so well regarded that he was invited to dinner at the White House.

Culture

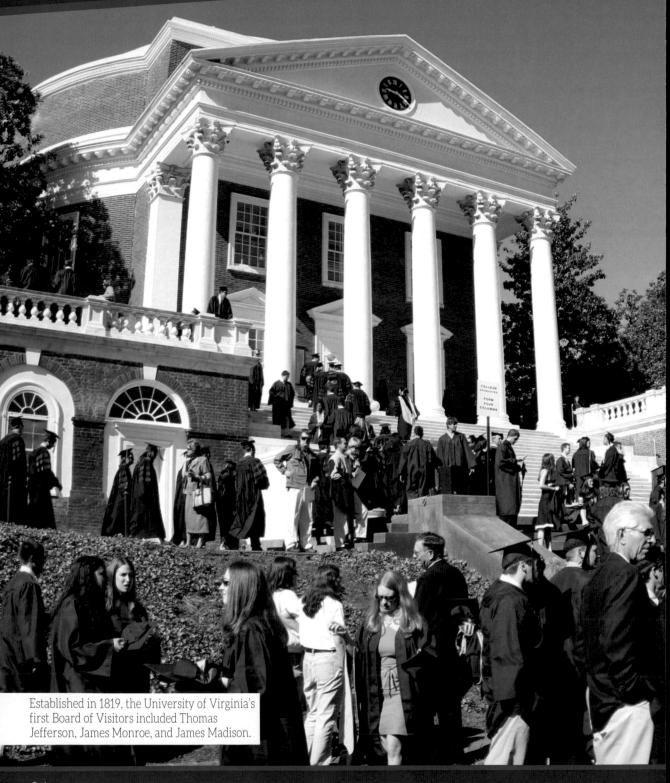

Established in 1819, the University of Virginia's first Board of Visitors included Thomas Jefferson, James Monroe, and James Madison.

Charlottesville is the home of more than 49,000 Virginians. The median age of residents is 28.1.

The People Today

The 2010 census counted more than 8 million people in the Old Dominion. The state population grew by 13 percent between 2000 and 2010. Growth was especially rapid in northern Virginia, which includes the counties near Washington, D.C. This region, which is home to one of every four Virginia residents, experienced a 23 percent population increase during the decade.

About 70 percent of the state's population is of European ancestry. Many people have British, German, or Irish heritage. The state has a higher percentage of African Americans than the national average and a smaller proportion of Hispanic Americans.

More than 7 of every 10 Virginians live in cities or towns. Some of these places are part of the Washington, D.C., metropolitan area. The state has a highly educated workforce. Approximately 88 percent of Virginians over the age of 25 are high school graduates. About 35 percent of the state's citizens have a college or university degree.

The northern Virginia region has been growing much more **rapidly** than the state as a whole.

Q What are some reasons people would want to move to northern Virginia?

Virginia's state capitol is more than 225 years old. In 1960, it was deemed a National Historic Landmark.

State Government

Virginia's constitution divides the state government into executive, legislative, and judicial branches. The head of the executive branch is the governor, who is elected to a single four-year term and may not run for reelection. The governor has the power to approve or **veto** state laws. Other elected executive officials include the lieutenant governor and the attorney general, both of whom may serve an unlimited number of four-year terms.

The General Assembly is the state's lawmaking body, or legislature. It consists of the House of Delegates, with 100 members, and the Senate, with 40 members. Delegates are elected for two-year terms, and senators are elected for four-year terms. The judicial branch is the state's court system. The highest court is the Supreme Court. It consists of a chief justice and six other justices.

Virginia has 95 counties and 39 cities that are independent of county government. The state sends 11 representatives and 2 senators to the U.S. Congress. Virginia casts 13 electoral votes in presidential elections.

Terry McAuliffe served as the chairman of Hilary Clinton's 2008 election campaign. He became the 72nd governor of Virginia in 2014.

Virginia does not have an official state song. "Carry Me Back to Ol' Virginny," written by James A. Bland, was the state song from 1940 through the mid-1990s. Many people came to regard the racial language and attitudes in the song as outdated and offensive. In 1997, the General Assembly voted to make it "state song emeritus." This meant that the song, while honored for its history, would be retired and no longer played on public occasions.

The Virginia state capitol is home to the Virginia General Assembly, the oldest legislative body in the Western Hemisphere.

The African American Cultural Arts Festival, featuring music and dance, has been celebrated in Charlottesville, Virginia since 1989.

Celebrating Culture

The first Africans arrived in the Virginia colony in 1619. The expansion of tobacco growing in the colony led to a rise in the demand for African slave labor. By 1860, on the eve of the Civil War, nearly 500,000 African American slaves were living in the state. The war put an end to slavery, but the state passed new laws intended to make African Americans legally and economically inferior to whites.

In the 1950s, when the U.S. Supreme Court outlawed racially **segregated** public schools, many public schools in the Old Dominion were closed in order to prevent this desegregation. In 1965, the state ended school segregation, and in 1989, state voters elected Virginia's first African American governor, Douglas Wilder. Each February, during Black History Month, events throughout the state recall the history of African Americans in Virginia, as well as African American contributions to the nation's early history.

The kilted bagpipers at the annual Scottish Christmas Parade in Alexandria celebrate Virginia's Scots-Irish culture. The Scotch-Irish came to the state when thousands of immigrants traveled through the Shenandoah Valley in the 1700s.

Many Virginia festivals celebrate the state's colonial history and the lives of the early European settlers. The Frontier Culture Museum near Staunton has exhibits that show what life was like for the early settlers. The Virginia First Thanksgiving Festival is held each year at Berkeley Plantation and features re-creations of the original celebration, including crafts, music, and food.

Native American culture is celebrated throughout Virginia. Each May, Clarksville is the site of the annual Native American Heritage Festival and Powwow. It features Native American arts, songs, and dances.

The culture and traditions of early Native Americans in Virginia are preserved by their descendants at annual powwows.

The Virginia Museum of Fine Arts is one of the largest art museums in North America.

Arts and Entertainment

The arts have a long history of support in Virginia. The state-supported Virginia Museum of Fine Arts opened in Richmond in 1936. Virginia's capital city also has a symphony orchestra and a ballet company. The Virginia Opera presents productions in Richmond, Norfolk, and Fairfax. One of the state's newest museums is the Taubman Museum of Art in Roanoke. Notable theaters in Virginia include the Barter Theatre in Abingdon and the American Shakespeare Center in Staunton.

Virginia has produced many well-known writers. The Pulitzer Prize–winning novelist Willa Cather was born near Winchester. Her works include *O Pioneers!*, *My Antonia*, *One of Ours*, and *Death Comes for the Archbishop*. Tom Wolfe, a Richmond native, wrote acclaimed works such as *The Bonfire of the Vanities* and *The Right Stuff*.

Built in 1919, the **Attucks Theater** in Norfolk, Virginia is the **oldest theater** built and run by African Americans.

The **Edgar Allan Poe Museum** opened in Richmond in 1922 to document and celebrate the writer's life.

Two talented female vocalists had ties to the city of Newport News. Jazz singer Ella Fitzgerald was internationally known as the "First Lady of Song," while Pearl Bailey became known as a star of stage, screen, and nightclubs. Winchester was the home city of Patsy Cline, an all-time great in the field of country music. Cline was the first female solo performer to enter the Country Music Hall of Fame. The Carter Family and Roy Clark are two other famous country music acts from Virginia. Many famous bluegrass musicians are associated with the state, including the Virginia-born singer, banjo player, and bandleader Ralph Stanley.

Virginia native Ella Fitzgerald burst onto the Harlem jazz scene in the 1930s at the age of 17. She had one of the most successful careers in music history.

Ralph Stanley began playing bluegrass in 1946. He is considered part of the first generation of bluegrass musicians and has been inducted into the International Bluegrass Music Hall of Honor.

Sports and Recreation

Hot air balloons operate outside of Richmond, offering sweeping views of Virginia's landscape.

Virginia's rivers, lakes, forests, mountains, and coastal areas offer a variety of recreational opportunities. Camping, hiking, hunting, boating, and fishing are popular in the state, especially in national forests and state parks. Lake Anna and Smith Mountain Lake cater to boating enthusiasts. The James, Shenandoah, and Maury Rivers attract kayakers and canoeists. Fishers need licenses to catch the many varieties of bass, trout, pike, and other freshwater fish in the state. Virginia is also an excellent location for saltwater fishing.

More than **400 golf courses** are located in Virginia, and the Homestead Resort's Cascades course is considered one of the best in the United States.

More than 500 miles of trails and 11 swimming beaches make Virginia's **36 state parks** and **62 natural areas** popular locations for recreation.

Several former rail routes have been adapted for use by hikers, cyclists, and horseback riders. The New River Trail is a 52-mile rail bed between Galax and Pulaski. The Virginia Creeper Trail, between Abingdon and Whitetop, is 34 miles long. Hikers also use the 550-mile portion of the Appalachian Trail that winds through Virginia.

The Shenandoah Valley is known for its scenic drives and beautiful hiking trails.

Downhill skiing in Virginia is available at the Homestead, Bryce, Massanutten, and Wintergreen resorts. During the summer, Bryce Resort, in the Shenandoah Valley, also offers grass skiing and mountain boarding. Grass skiing actually uses skates instead of skis, and mountain boarding is like snowboarding on wheels.

Both recreational and competitive horseback riding are well established in Virginia. Every year, **steeplechase** fans watch to see who will win the Virginia Gold Cup Races. NASCAR fans head for stock-car auto racetracks at Richmond and Martinsville. In college sports, the Hokies of Virginia Tech have a wide following.

The Richmond International Raceway is one of NASCAR's premier racetracks. Each year, drivers compete in the Sprint Cup Series Federated Auto Parts 400 race.

Get To Know
VIRGINIA

When the Syms Free School was founded in Hampton in **1634**, it became the **first free public school** in the United States.

More than half of the battles during the Civil War were fought in Virginia.

MOUNT ROGERS IS THE HIGHEST POINT IN VIRGINIA, WITH AN ALTITUDE OF 5,729 FEET.

Yorktown is the site of the last victory of the **American Revolutionary War**.

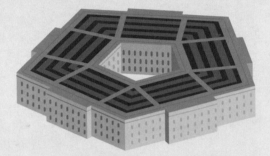

The Pentagon building is the **largest office building** in the world, by floor area.

The **Virginia Zoo**, in Norfolk, was founded as a park in 1899 and began to collect animals the following year. Today, animals in the zoo represent **115 different species**.

Virginia's **first newspaper** was the *Virginia Gazette*, which began publication in Williamsburg in **1736**.

Brain Teasers

What have you learned about Virginia after reading this book? Test your knowledge by answering these questions. All of the information can be found in the text you just read. The answers are provided below for easy reference.

1 Who was the first European to visit Virginia?

2 Monticello, a Virginia historical site and tourist attraction, was once the home of what U.S. president?

3 The Virginia economy began on the growing of what plant?

4 In what year did Virginia secede from the union?

5 The Native Americans in the Virginia area were members of what confederacy?

6 How many members are in the Virginia legislature, or General Assembly?

7 In what month is Black History Month celebrated?

8 Who was the first African American governor of Virginia?

Key Words

amphibians: animals that can live both on land and in water

archives: a collection of records and documents

broiler chickens: chickens raised for their meat rather than their eggs

civilian: a person who does not work for the military or the police

habitations: places to live

indentured servants: people bound to an employer for a set number of years

metropolitan area: a large city and its surrounding towns and suburbs

plantation: large farm usually worked by people who live on the property

ratify: give formal approval

seceded: separated from an organization or nation

segregated: racially separated and restricted

steeplechase: a horse race with obstacles such as ditches and hedges

veto: to reject a bill passed by the legislature

Index

Log on to www.av2books.com

AV² by Weigl brings you media enhanced books that support active learning. Go to www.av2books.com, and enter the special code found on page 2 of this book. You will gain access to enriched and enhanced content that supplements and complements this book. Content includes video, audio, weblinks, quizzes, a slide show, and activities.

AV² Online Navigation

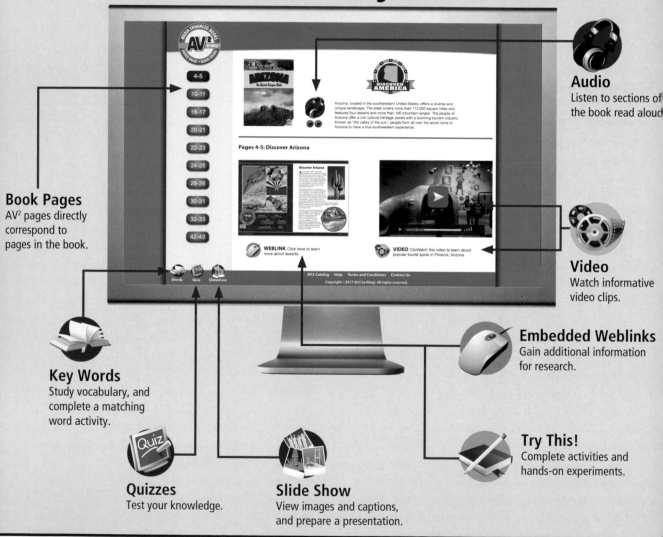

Audio
Listen to sections of the book read aloud.

Book Pages
AV² pages directly correspond to pages in the book.

Video
Watch informative video clips.

Key Words
Study vocabulary, and complete a matching word activity.

Embedded Weblinks
Gain additional information for research.

Try This!
Complete activities and hands-on experiments.

Quizzes
Test your knowledge.

Slide Show
View images and captions, and prepare a presentation.

AV² was built to bridge the gap between print and digital. We encourage you to tell us what you like and what you want to see in the future.

Sign up to be an AV² Ambassador at www.av2books.com/ambassador.

Due to the dynamic nature of the Internet, some of the URLs and activities provided as part of AV² by Weigl may have changed or ceased to exist. AV² by Weigl accepts no responsibility for any such changes. All media enhanced books are regularly monitored to update addresses and sites in a timely manner. Contact AV² by Weigl at 1-866-649-3445 or av2books@weigl.com with any questions, comments, or feedback.